The
FIRST BOOK
of
WORLD
WAR
I

The
FIRST BOOK
of

WORLD WAR I

by
LOUIS L. SNYDER

maps by
LEONARD DERWINSKI

FRANKLIN WATTS
NEW YORK

This book is for Meryl Ann Lieberman

Copyright © 1958 by Franklin Watts, Inc.

26 27 28 29 30

ISBN 0-531-00675-1
ISBN 0-531-02318-4 (pbk)

Printed in the United States of America

Library of Congress Catalog Card Number: 58-5813

PICTURE CREDITS

CONTENTS

THE SHOTS HEARD AROUND THE WORLD

It was June, 1914. At tables in a humble café in Bosnia, in the heart of the Balkans in Central Europe, sat thirty-five men. Most of them were young students. There were also teachers, tradesmen, peasants, and workers. All were from farms and towns of the small provinces of Bosnia and Herzegovina, which the great Austro-Hungarian Empire had taken from Serbia a few years earlier.

These men were terrorists, members of the secret Serbian society called the *Narodna Odbrana,* or National Defense, who had pledged themselves to work for freedom. Their meeting that night was in protest against the coming visit of the Austrian Archduke Francis Ferdinand to Sarajevo, capital of Bosnia. The Archduke planned to direct army maneuvers in the neighboring mountains.

The terrorists resented the coming display of armed might in their conquered land. They also resented its timing — June 28, which was *Vidov-Dan,* St. Vitus Day, the five hundred and twenty-fifth anniversary of Serbia's freedom from Turkish rule. They made their decision almost immediately. Death to the tyrant!

Later, eight members of the society were selected to carry out the sentence. They were to wait five hundred yards apart along the route the Archduke had to travel from the railroad station to the Town Hall. Among so many, one would surely succeed in killing him.

Among those chosen to kill the Archduke was a nineteen-year-old student, Gavrilo Princip. As a small boy he had tended sheep in Bosnia, where he had learned from the highland peasants the old folk

The Archduke Francis Ferdinand and his wife leaving the Town Hall at Sarajevo

tales and songs of Serbia's glorious past. Expelled from school at Sarajevo because of revolutionary activities, he had gone to Belgrade, capital of Serbia. Homeless, ill, and often hungry, he was kept alive only by his hope of leading his people to freedom.

At dawn on June 28 the eight conspirators were armed and waiting along the route. When the Archduke appeared, one of them hurled a grenade at his car. The Archduke threw himself back and was not injured. After the reception at the Town Hall he was urged to leave by the shortest route out of the city.

As the Archduke's car turned at the bridge over the River Miljachka, Princip stepped forward and fired two shots. One pierced the Archduke's neck so that blood spurted from his mouth. The other struck the Archduke's wife, who died instantly. The Archduke's last words were, "Sophie, Sophie, do not die! Live for our children!"

The officers seized Princip. They knocked him down, beat him with their swords, all but killed him. The boy died in prison, but his shots echoed around the world to set off the explosion of World War I.

WHAT CAUSED WORLD WAR I

The causes of great wars are never simple. Many causes may work quietly under the surface for years before they are recognized. In 1914 nobody dreamed that a great war would spread from Europe all over the world. The continent seemed more stable than it had been for centuries. But under the calm seethed old rivalries, suspicions, and hatreds. They were ready to erupt for the slightest reason. To understand them we must go way back to the late nineteenth century.

At that time the nations of Europe were engaged in a fierce struggle for raw materials and markets for their products. Some nations managed to get these at the expense of others. Many nations needed food supplies. And the bankers in every country wanted places to invest their money.

From this struggle Great Britain (England) had emerged as the strongest power in the world. Her industries and commerce were greater than those of any other nation. Her colonial empire was first in size and importance. Her navy ruled the seas.

But at the beginning of the twentieth century the picture began to change. Germany became a dangerous contestant in shipping and commerce. Largely because of her efficiency and scientific genius she began to outstrip Great Britain in the production of coal, iron, and steel. The rivalry between these two great countries grew strong and bitter.

While the struggle for markets and raw materials was at its height, an evil spirit began to grow in some of the countries of Europe — a

9

spirit that drew them apart from their neighbors. It was the spirit of bad nationalism.

Good nationalism hurts nobody. It is a feeling that binds together people who live in the same country, speak the same language, and have similar customs and ideas. But the nationalism that began to spread in Europe during the late nineteenth century was like a crippling disease. The nations suffering from it began to feel superior to others and to covet the land of neighboring countries. Some were even ready to go to war to get what they wanted.

By 1914 this bad nationalism had produced many "sore spots" in the world. One of them was Alsace-Lorraine, the rich industrial region between Germany and France. Germany and France had fought over Alsace-Lorraine for a thousand years. Germany had won it in the war of 1870-1871. Now France wanted it back.

Then there was the great Austro-Hungarian monarchy, where Austrians and Hungarians were the favored people. The other subjects — among them Czechs, Poles, Serbians, and Rumanians — wanted to break away and form their own nations or join other states.

The people of Italy were dissatisfied, too. They believed that Fiume and Trieste, then under Austrian control, and Nice and Savoy, then part of France, were really Italian.

Poland was not even on the map in 1914. In the late eighteenth century it had been split up three times between Russia, Austria, and Prussia. But the feeling of Polish nationalism had never died. All over Europe there were people who still spoke Polish and had Polish customs. They wanted their country back.

EUROPE, 1914

ALLIED POWERS

CENTRAL POWERS

NEUTRALS

Italy joined the Allies in 1915

11

Along with bad nationalism, still another deadly disease infected Europe. This was militarism. Each country, fearful that war would break out, began to arm and prepare for war. The people were heavily taxed to pay for these preparations, and they resented it.

Restless and uneasy, the nations of Europe began to combine in a series of alliances — treaties between two or more nations — to work together if war came. In 1882 Germany, Austria-Hungary, and Italy formed the secret Triple Alliance.

There was no world government, such as the United Nations today, to help solve the quarrels between nations. The only way to stop a country that broke the laws of nations was to go to war against it. In 1899 and later, in 1907, there were Peace Conferences at The Hague that tried to do something about this. They failed. The nations agreed on rules of land and naval warfare, the rights of neutrals, and the handling of prisoners of war, but they were not able to prevent the outbreak of war on a giant scale.

Diplomacy, the relations between nations, became a kind of trickery. A diplomat was said to be a man "who lied for his country." Sworn allies were not necessarily loyal friends. In some cases nations even made secret agreements with the enemies of their allies.

In 1905 trouble flared in Morocco. Germany wanted part of that country, but France objected. War was barely avoided.

France, Russia, and Great Britain had strong suspicions that Germany was preparing for war. Although they had been enemies for years, these three countries decided that they must get together for protection. In 1907 they formed their own alliance, calling it the Triple Entente. It was not secret, however. France and Great Britain were countries in which treaties had to be made publicly by their Parliaments — the Chamber of Deputies (France) and the House of Commons (Great Britain).

Now Europe was divided into two great hostile camps, with the Triple Alliance on one side and the Triple Entente on the other. With suspicion growing and tensions tightening, it was anybody's guess who would fire the first shot.

In the Balkans, known as the "powder keg of Europe," there had been continuous friction for years. Greece, Serbia, Montenegro, and Bulgaria all wanted Turkey driven out of her possessions in southeastern Europe. In 1912 they went to war against Turkey and won. Then they began to fight among themselves for the best pieces of Turkey.

You can see that Europe was well primed for the explosion set off by Gavrilo Princip's shots at Sarajevo.

13

←
Kaiser Wilhelm II (left) with his six sons leads a military parade in Berlin

THE CRISIS OF JULY, 1914

The Austro-Hungarian Foreign Minister, Count Leopold von Berchtold, was a good deal to blame for what happened next. He was furious with the Serbs for the murder of the Archduke, and he was eager to strike back at them. The German Kaiser, Wilhelm II, agreed that the Serbs deserved a lesson. He promised to support Austria-Hungary in anything she did to punish them. Like many others, the Kaiser believed that if Serbia resisted, the conflict could be kept between Austria-Hungary and Serbia.

On July 23, 1914, Count Berchtold sent Serbia a diplomatic note so harsh that it was actually an ultimatum, or final demand. It insisted on punishment for all those who had taken part in the plot. It demanded that Austrian police officials be allowed to go into Serbia to see that this was done. In short, Serbia was to give up her rights as an independent state. The ultimatum further called for a reply within forty-eight hours.

For the Serbs this was a deadly serious matter. They now asked for advice from two friendly states, France and Russia. Both urged Serbia to send a moderate reply to the ultimatum.

On July 25, just two minutes short of the time limit, the Serbs sent their answer. They accepted all the demands except the one specifying that Austrian officials be sent into Serbia.

"We cannot accept your note," said Count Berchtold. "It is unsatisfactory."

On July 28, Austria-Hungary declared war on Serbia.

At this point the Russians began to mobilize their armies. In those days mobilization was a dangerous word. It meant that armies were ordered to be ready to fight at an instant's notice. It was the next thing to a declaration of war.

Both British and German leaders begged the Russians not to mobilize. They also urged the Austrians to accept a peaceful solution. But it was too late. Soon the would-be peacemakers found themselves in the midst of the fight.

Germany declared war on Russia on August 1. Two days later Germany declared war on France. France, honoring her treaty with Russia, promptly declared war on Germany and Austria-Hungary. Italy held aloof. She said she was not bound to help Germany because Germany had started the war. With the withdrawal of Italy from the Triple Alliance, Germany and Austria-Hungary became known as the Central Powers.

French soldiers, in their picturesque uniforms, on their way to join their regiments

THE INVASION OF BELGIUM

The Germans had a well-thought-out plan for winning the war quickly. First they would overwhelm the French with superior numbers. Then they would turn against the Russians. While holding the Russians in the East they would head for a knockout blow on Paris. The attack would be like a gigantic hammer with all the force in its head.

To carry out their plan to attack Paris, the Germans would have to swing in a wide arc through Belgium, which lies between Germany and France. Back in 1839 all the great states of Europe had signed a treaty guaranteeing the neutrality of that little country. In case a great war broke out, the warring armies would not enter Belgian territory.

Now one of the German leaders called this treaty "a scrap of paper." On August 4, the German armies surged across the Belgian border.

A famous American war correspondent, Richard Harding Davis, was in Brussels, the capital of Belgium, the day the Germans goose-stepped through. He wrote an unforgettable story about it for the New York *Tribune*:

"... The German army moved into this city as smoothly and as compactly as an Empire State Express. There were no halts, no open places, no stragglers. . . .

"It came in with the smoke pouring from cookstoves on wheels, and in an hour had set up postoffice wagons, from which mounted messengers galloped along the line of column distributing letters and at which soldiers posted picture postcards. . . .

The German army
marches into Brussels,
capital of Belgium, August, 1914

"The men of the infantry sang *Fatherland, My Fatherland*. Between each line of song they took three steps. At times two thousand men were singing together in absolute rhythm and beat. When the melody gave way the silence was broken only by the stamp of iron-shod boots, and then again the song rose. . . .

"Like a river of steel the army flowed, gray and ghostlike. Then, as dusk came and as thousands of horses' hoofs and thousands of iron boots continued to tramp forward, they struck tiny sparks from the stones, but the horses and the men who beat out the sparks were invisible. . . .

"Whether they marched all night or not I do not know, but now for twenty-six hours the gray army has rumbled by with the mystery of fog and the pertinacity of a steam roller."

17

The little Belgian army resisted fiercely, but it was no match for this monstrous German army of death. Tiny Belgium was overcome within two weeks.

Shocked by this disregard of international law, England immediately declared war on the Central Powers. Now the two great alliances were at war with each other.

Japan came to the support of England on August 23. One nation after another was drawn into the fighting. What had started as a little war in the Balkans now spread into a world conflict.

A German girl bids a gay farewell to a soldier leaving for the war

WAR FEVER

"The lights are going out all over Europe," said Sir Edward Grey, British Secretary for Foreign Affairs, just before the war began.

Yet in all the warring capitals the people seemed relieved that the strain of the armed peace was broken. Men, women, and children in every land were swept along in an outburst of patriotism. Newspapers and politicians shrieked that "our country" was the innocent victim of attack by the hated enemy.

Berlin was afire with war fever. People thronged the streets shouting, "War! War!" German troops goose-stepped down Unter den Linden to the tune of fierce Teutonic warrior songs. Girls kissed the blushing soldiers and put flowers in their guns.

Joyful crowds surged down the boulevards in Paris as shouts arose, "To Berlin! To Berlin!" Parisians massed in the Place de la Concorde and sang battle anthems. Speakers called for revenge for 1870-1871, when the Germans had beaten France.

19

Belgian soldiers retreating toward the one little corner of Belgium which soon would be the only part of Belgium outside the German lines

In Piccadilly Circus, London crowds sang and shouted, "Death to the Hun!" British troops, marching to the tune of "Tipperary," set out as on a holiday.

In Russia, tough peasants abandoned their plows and headed for the cities to join the army. In St. Petersburg (later in 1924, Leningrad), mobs attacked the German embassy and called for victory for Mother Russia. A prize of 200,000 rubles ($100,000) was set up for the first Russian soldier to set foot in Berlin.

Everything seemed glamorous at the time. Boys and girls were told that it was a fine and noble thing to die for one's country. The war, they were promised, would be short and glorious, like those of the nineteenth century.

It was a tragic mistake. People in 1914 knew nothing of modern war.

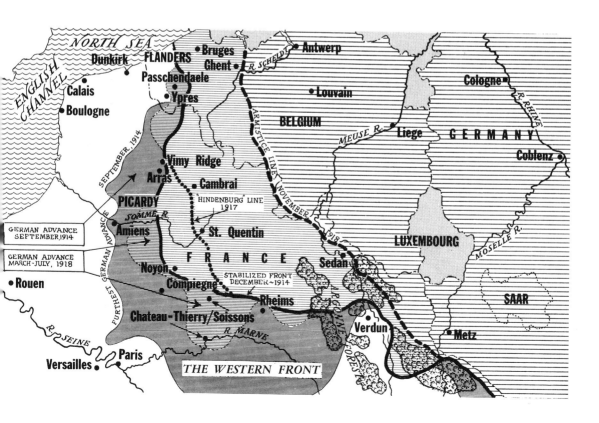

THE WESTERN FRONT

THE MIRACLE OF THE MARNE

"In six weeks it will all be over."

This was the telegram which General Helmuth von Moltke sent to Kaiser Wilhelm II after the invasion of Belgium.

A million German troops had poured into France. Despite the arrival of a British unit and French reinforcements, the Germans pushed steadily forward. Sometimes they marched as much as twenty miles a day on foot.

Unfortunately for them, the Germans tried too much too quickly. In those days messages between units of the army were carried by men on horseback and motorcyclists. Many of these messengers lost their way in the confusion of the advance. Besides, the Germans had made the mistake of destroying all French telegraphic lines and stations. Often German field commanders lost touch with each other and with their headquarters.

In the midst of the confusion, General von Moltke received an urgent message from East Prussia, saying that the Russians were pouring in, and begging for help. He promptly transferred four of his divisions to the East. It was a serious mistake.

In spite of the confusion, however, the Germans reached the river Marne, fifteen miles from Paris, in the first week of September. The French government fled to Bordeaux, and the French and British staged a desperate counterattack. General Joseph Joffre, in charge of the French troops, said to his men, "The time for looking backward has passed. Die in your tracks rather than retreat!"

21

The famous First Battle of the Marne lasted five days, from September 6 to 10. Two million men were gripped in a battle to the death. It seemed that the Germans were about to win. The French commanders called for help from Paris.

Then an amazing thing happened. From the streets of Paris came a long line of taxicabs and buses, headed for the front. Piled into this strange fleet were troops gathered from around Paris.

Suddenly the tide of battle turned in favor of the Allies. The Germans could scarcely believe it. For four weeks they had rolled on through Belgium and France. Now they had hit a stone wall. They halted and retreated in orderly fashion to the Aisne River. The six weeks were over. The Germans, although in a dominant position, had failed to reach their goal. Their hope for a quick victory had vanished.

WAR IN THE TRENCHES

After the German drive on Paris had been stopped, both sides dug into the ground. The fire power of the machine gun and the field gun was so great that no man could stand up against it. The troops, like moles, had to seek protection under the ground.

There was nothing new about the simple trench. Caesar had used it against the Gauls. And both the North and the South had dug trenches in the American Civil War. What was new was the *use* of trenches on a grand scale.

First, each side dug a long line of trenches underground, stretching nearly six hundred miles from Belgium down to Switzerland. But a single trench system did not offer much protection. So both sides made second and third line trenches to which its troops could retreat if they could not hold the first line.

All these lines were connected underground so that the soldiers could move from one line to another without being exposed to enemy fire. Under the ground were first-aid stations, troops' and officers' quarters, kitchens, supply depots, even miniature cars running on rails.

Between the German and Allied trenches was "No Man's Land." It was covered with mounds of dirt and tangles of barbed wire. It was a dangerous place in which to be caught, because it was continually swept by gunfire of all kinds.

Day after day, week after week, the opposing armies lived in the water, muck, and mud of these trenches. In the summer it was blasted

←

Buses and taxicabs which carried French troops to the front during the First Battle of the Marne

hot, in the winter cold and wet. The trenches were infested with vermin, especially by vigorous insects called "cooties."

During the day the ground trembled with the concussion of the heavy guns. Men's ears ached with the incessant bark of these big guns with their deep-throated bass. Then came the rattle of the machine guns, each delivering three hundred shots a minute.

At night the battlefront was lit up by huge flares. Every few seconds came the flashes of the big guns. Giant fireworks exploded in the air and made the scene as bright as day.

During the night it was time for the rats to take over. They swarmed

"No Man's Land"

in and out of the dugouts and jumped over the heads of the men while they slept.

Just before the break of dawn, soldiers waited at the edge of the trench for the signal to "go over the top." Knowing they stood small chance of coming out of "No Man's Land" alive, they were usually in a cold sweat. But orders were orders, and they had to go to the attack. Sometimes the enemy trench was only ten yards away.

Worst of all were the unceasing monotony and boredom. Nobody could make much headway against the combination of trenches, machine guns, and barbed wire. Both sides tried to blast their way through by heavy artillery bombardments, but it was really impossible to make any major attacks against the enemy. Yet the commanders of both sides insisted upon hurling their men against positions which just could not be taken. It seemed that no one could get anywhere unless one side developed new weapons.

The faces of these men mirror the misery of life.
in the trenches on the Western Front

THE RACE TO THE SEA

In October the Germans and the Allies began a series of attempts to outflank each other and occupy the ports on the English Channel. It was a "race to the sea." If the Germans won, they could seriously interfere with British aid to France.

During the first two weeks of October the Germans captured one Belgian city after another — Ghent, Bruges, Ostend, Zeebrugge, and Antwerp. At last the Allies stopped them in Flanders, a little corner in western Belgium and northeastern France. Here, in the town of Ypres, called "Wipers," by the British Tommies, or soldiers, the terrible First Battle of Ypres took place. One British division entered it with four hundred officers and twelve thousand men. It came out of the slaughter with only 44 officers and 2,336 men! Thousands were buried at Flanders. A sensitive poet, John McCrae, wrote, "In Flanders fields the poppies blow, between the crosses row on row."

There followed one of the greatest examples of heroism in the history of war. For four long years the British held on to Flanders. The Germans held all the high ground. The British troops had no way to conceal themselves in the dismal lowlands. They had to dig holes and crawl into them, and the holes usually filled up with water. During the winters the Tommies were up to their knees in mud, or stood waist-high in icy water.

But the British "stuck it." For the rest of the war they held onto this important strip of Belgium and also controlled the French cities of Calais, Dunkirk, and Boulogne.

Russian Cossacks in East Prussia

THE WAR IN THE EAST

As soon as war was declared, the massed Russian armies moved into East Prussia and headed for the city of Königsberg. Under the sweltering August sun they swept across the sandy soil. The dreaded Cossacks, Russian fighters on horseback, charged through the countryside, driving panic-stricken peasants before them with whips and swords. Tales of Cossack brutality seeped back to Berlin, inflaming the German hatred of the Russians.

The Russian armies were under the command of General Alexei Samsonov and General Pavel Karlovich Rennenkampf, who hated each other. Each wanted the honor of leading his troops first into Berlin. And each kept from the other the whereabouts of his army. It was a strange way to fight a war!

The Germans did not have as many troops as the Russians, but they had an excellent railroad system. More, they had brilliant military leadership. The German commanders were General Paul von Hindenburg, the 67-year-old war horse, and General Erich Ludendorff. Ludendorff was a Bavarian staff officer who had shown his courage in taking the fortresses of Belgium at the start of the war.

Hindenburg and Ludendorff had a daring plan. They would take on Samsonov's and Rennenkampf's armies separately, one after the other.

The plan worked. Between August 23 and 31, 1914, the Germans destroyed Samsonov's army in the Battle of Tannenberg. A week later,

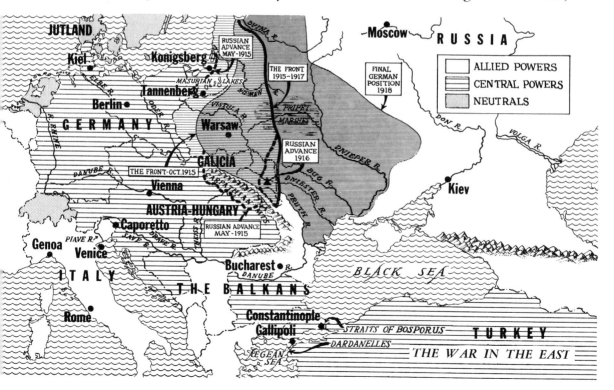

railroad trains carried the German forces northward to their second victory. Here, at the Battle of the Masurian Lakes, they defeated Rennenkampf.

It was a disastrous defeat for the Russians. They lost a vast amount of war materials. Two-thirds of their invading divisions were destroyed. Now they were thrown on the defensive.

General von Hindenburg was hailed as a national savior. In Berlin the Germans erected a huge wooden statue of their hero. Boys and girls who paid a few marks were allowed to drive an iron nail into the statue. Soon it stood gleaming brightly in the sun.

It was because of the victories at Tannenberg and the Masurian Lakes that Hindenburg and Ludendorff later became supreme warlords in Germany.

Against their other enemies the Russians were more successful. They drove the defenders of Austrian Galicia back to the Carpathian Mountains. The Austrians had to send so many of their troops to fight the Russians that they were unable to conquer Serbia. On December 2, 1914, they managed to take Belgrade, but they held it for only a few weeks. The hated "pig farmers of Serbia" struck back fiercely. But they were not strong enough to regain Bosnia and Herzegovina, where the war had started.

Fighting in the East was a seesaw affair, with neither side gaining or losing very much. Gradually it settled down to trench warfare, as it had in the West. At the end of 1914 the opposing armies in the East faced each other in a deadlock along a front some 1,900 miles long — the longest battle line in history.

SEA WARFARE IN 1914

Because neither side had struck a knockout blow on land, sea warfare became important early in the war.

Huge battleships were the backbone of navies in World War I. At the start of the war the British had 55 battleships, the French 21, the Germans 33, and Austria-Hungary 13. Great Britain ruled the waves with overwhelming power.

Britain's first task was to clear the Mediterranean Sea of enemy surface craft. She did this. In August, 1914, she trapped two German cruisers, the *Goeben* and the *Breslau,* in the Mediterranean. They escaped, however, and made a run for friendly Turkish waters.

Second, and even more important, the British navy closed the routes from the North Sea to the Atlantic to German shipping. Britain's aim was to blockade Germany and prevent any food or war materials from reaching her from across the seas. The blockade caused great bitterness not only in Germany but also in those countries that were not at war. British warships made all neutral ships come to British ports to be searched for contraband — anything that could be used for war.

The British navy was successful in this task. Within a week after the fighting started, it had either captured or driven into neutral waters nearly every German merchant ship afloat.

The Germans knew that they had to break the blockade which was slowly strangling them. They had a large food supply, but not enough. Moreover, before long they would exhaust their stocks of oil, rubber, gasoline, and cotton, all vital war materials.

German forts at Heligoland in the North Sea

While they kept their battlefleet at home, the Germans used mines and U-boats (undersea boats), commonly called submarines, to fight the British blockade. In September, 1914, a German U-boat sank three old British cruisers. It was the biggest single strike of the war.

At this time two German cruisers, the *Gneisenau* and the *Scharnhorst,* were in the Pacific. They made for home around Cape Horn, the southernmost point of South America. They were like two foxes being chased by a merciless pack of hounds, the British fleet. The British caught them and sent them to the bottom in the Battle of the Falkland Islands on December 8, 1914.

General Paul von Hindenburg, Kaiser William II, and General Erich Ludendorff trace the progress of the war on a table map

THE WAR IN ASIA AND AFRICA

In 1914 Japan, allied with Great Britain, attacked and occupied Kiao-chau, a district in northeast China. Kiao-chau was the great German stronghold in the Far East. That was the only part Japan took in the war, except for patrolling the Pacific to protect British ships against German attack.

In the early months of the war, British and French colonial armies attacked and occupied the German colonies of Togo and the Cameroons in Africa. In 1915, South African armies under command of General Jan Smuts conquered German Southwest Africa. In German East Africa, British, Portuguese, and Belgian colonial troops fought against a small force of Germans leading native soldiers.

Having lost command of the seas, the Germans saw their colonial empire pass into the hands of the Allies.

DISASTER AT GALLIPOLI

At the outbreak of the war, Turkey had been neutral. But the Allies knew that she sympathized with the Germans. On November 3, 1914, Russia had declared war on Turkey. Two days later Great Britain and France did the same.

In order to trade munitions and guns with Russia for badly needed grains, the Allies decided early in 1915 that they would have to capture Constantinople. Winston Churchill, then First Lord of the Admiralty, argued for a combined naval-land attack at Gallipoli. If Turkey were defeated, he said, the war could be shortened by two years.

Now let us pretend for a few moments that we are armchair strategists, amateur generals. It's a safe way to fight a war!

Turn back to the map of Europe on page 11 and look for the Black Sea in the East. This big inland sea is between Russia and Turkey. For centuries the Russians have been trying to get out from that sea into the warm water of the Mediterranean. They have only cold-water ports in the north which freeze over in winter.

If a Russian ship tries to get to the Mediterranean from the Black Sea, it must first pass through the Straits of Bosporus separating Europe from Asia. On the shores of the Straits is the Turkish city of Constantinople (now called Istanbul), the famous old gateway to the markets of the Orient. Then the ship comes into the inland Sea of Marmora. Next it must pass through the Straits of the Dardanelles, on the north side of which is the peninsula of Gallipoli. Finally it must dodge all the islands of the Aegean Sea to get into the Mediterranean Sea.

If you reverse the process, you will see that it is just as hard to bring a ship from the Mediterranean to the Black Sea and Russia.

On February 19, 1915, a powerful Anglo-French fleet of about one hundred ships, headed by the super-dreadnought *Queen Elizabeth,* appeared at the entrance of the Dardanelles. The great naval guns boomed and soon silenced the guns of the Turkish forts guarding the entrance.

The Allied fleet now sailed into the Narrows of the Dardanelles. Here they met disaster. Floating mines worked havoc among the warships. From the shores heavy German Krupp guns poured fire on the invaders. Several ships were lost. The fleet withdrew.

Obviously the Dardanelles could not be forced without the aid of land forces. An army went ashore under the command of Sir Ian Hamilton. There were British and French troops, French Senegalese, Ghurka regiments, and Anzacs (Australian and New Zealand Army Corps). Altogether, some five hundred thousand fighting men were brought ashore on this tongue of rock and scrub.

The invaders fought gallantly in hand-to-hand struggles and fierce onslaughts. They could not capture the fortified hills which commanded the plains. The combination of Turkish defenders, German guns, heat, flies, and dysentery was just too much for them. After a campaign lasting nearly nine months, the Allies gave up their precarious toe-hold in Gallipoli. Not until later did they learn the heartbreaking news that they were within a few inches of victory. The Turks had been about to withdraw!

It was a costly and tragic defeat, Britain's greatest failure of the war.

One of the first gas masks

POISON GAS

It was April 22, 1915. The British Tommies at Ypres in western Belgium were uncomfortable and wet in their little foxholes. Suddenly a mysterious cloud appeared, coming right toward them. Men everywhere began to collapse. Some grasped their throats as they coughed and choked to death. Others saved themselves by burying their faces in the earth or by stuffing handkerchiefs into their mouths.

This was the first important gas attack in history. The Germans were using chlorine, a deadly gas which harms nose, throat and lungs. Its use was against the Geneva Conventions, which had tried to set up rules to make war as humane as possible.

The Allies quickly devised defensive measures against the German gas. At first the troops dipped cotton pads in a neutralizing chemical solution and tied them over their mouths. Later, each soldier was issued a gas mask, which filtered out the poisonous gas from the air he breathed.

The Germans began using other kinds of poison gas, too, such as mustard or phosgene gas. But they became discouraged when the Allies started to return gas for gas. Their new weapon did not bring the Germans the quick victory for which they had hoped.

German fighter plane

WAR IN THE AIR

The English pilot in a little two-winged biplane pushed out of a cloud at top speed — a little over 100 miles an hour. Below him he spotted a plane with a German cross on its wings. Swooping down, he emptied all the chambers of his revolver at the German pilot. The shots didn't help much, but somehow the enemy plane began to stagger crazily.

As the Englishman flew by, he lifted his goggles and gallantly waved his hand at his opponent. The German saluted back as his plane spun to the ground.

Air combat in the early days of World War I was a personal fight between two "knights of the air." At first both sides used rickety little planes for scattering propaganda leaflets and similar planes to discover enemy positions or to direct artillery fire. The pilots had to fly high and try to remain unobserved.

Then in May, 1915, a twenty-five-year-old Dutchman, Anthony Fokker, invented a machine gun that could fire bullets from planes without striking the propeller blades. With this invention the Germans ruled the skies for a year. But soon the Allies came back with equal or even better guns on their planes.

Single combat gave way to battles between organized squadrons, which consisted of about ten to twenty planes each. When the flight leader of a British squadron sighted an enemy squadron, he gave a signal. All the planes went helter-skelter in every direction. It was each pilot for himself in these "dog fights."

There were many tricks of aerial acrobatics — the Immelmann turn, the side-slip, the nose-spin, and others. The idea was to get behind and just below the tail of an enemy plane. There the attacking pilot could not be reached by enemy fire and was well placed to get in a burst of fire at close range.

The feats of courage in these air duels were extraordinary. Any pilot who shot down at least five enemy planes was called an "ace." Captain Eddie Rickenbacker, a famous American ace, shot down 26 German planes in the brief time he was at the front. René Fonck and Charles Guynemer were distinguished French aces. Baron Manfred von Richtofen, called the Red Knight, leader of the German Flying Circus, shot down 80 Allied planes before he lost his life to a 24-year-old Canadian pilot, Roy Brown.

Later in the war, planes were used to attack enemy cities. The first daylight raid on London came in June, 1917. Thereafter, the city was protected by a balloon apron, barrage fire, and the Royal Air Force.

A "great" raid on London took place on May 19, 1918. Between thirty and forty German *Gothas* took part in the attack. But only forty-eight Londoners were killed. Others were injured. The Ger-

An aerial "dog fight" between German and Allied planes

mans lost seven planes — three shot down in air combat, three destroyed by gunfire from the ground, and one downed by engine failure. The German planes did not come back to London again during World War I.

The Germans also experimented with another kind of airship, the Zeppelin, invented in 1898 by Count Ferdinand von Zeppelin, a retired German army officer. The Zeppelin had a long aluminum hull covered with a weatherproof fabric. It was filled with hydrogen, a lighter-than-air gas. The German government spent huge sums in developing the Zeppelin, believing it could be used as a silent raider to bomb the British into submission.

On a night in spring, 1915, the great sprawling wartime city of London was blacked out. Suddenly the sirens began to sound. Shouts echoed through the streets.

"The Zeppelins are coming! The Zeppelins are coming!"

High over the city a dozen gigantic shadows, like huge cigars, came floating through the air. From them rained a hail of bombs. People scattered for cover. Searchlights pointed fingers of light directly at several of the monsters. Planes took off to attack them. Anti-aircraft guns began to rattle.

The Zeppelins finished their errand of death and drifted silently away, disappearing into the mist.

But the Zeppelins proved to have serious weaknesses. They were large, and could be attacked successfully by ground fire and airplanes. Filled with hydrogen gas, they caught fire easily. They could fly no faster than fifty-four miles an hour. And they were hard to control in rough weather.

As for the German plan of striking terror in the hearts of Englishmen, it just did not work. The British do not scare easily. In both world wars their courage under air attack aroused the admiration of the entire world.

After forty-eight Zeppelin raids on England, most of them against London, the Germans became discouraged. Too many of their gas bags were shot down. Once again the Germans had failed to find the secret weapons that would bring them a quick victory.

Artist's conception of a British fighter plane attacking a Zeppelin over London

Allied propaganda poster, portraying German atrocities in Belgium

THE BATTLE OF PROPAGANDA

World War I was the first great conflict in history in which whole nations went to war. It was a war not only of professional soldiers but of civilians doing their part on farms, of factories making war materials, of civil defense duties. Everybody, in one way or another, took part in it.

Both sides had to be convinced that they were fighting a just war and that the enemy had to be destroyed. For the first time governments used propaganda, a means of influencing people's thoughts and emotions, on a large scale.

The propagandists used whatever served them best — slogans, speeches, newspaper and magazine articles, pictures. In Vienna a business firm printed propaganda photographs that could be used by either side!

Some of the German propaganda slogans were:

"God Punish England."

"On to Paris."

"Germany Above All."

And here are some British slogans:

"England Expects Every Man to Do His Duty."

"King and Country Need You."

"God Speed the Plow and the Woman Who Drives It."

"More Men and Still More Until the Enemy Is Crushed."

To create hatred for the enemy, the Germans had a popular song called the *Hasslied,* or "Song of Hate:"

> "French and Russian they matter not,
> A blow for a blow and a shot for a shot. . . .
> We will never forego our hate,
> We have but one single hate,
> We love as one, we hate as one,
> We have one foe, and one alone —
> ENGLAND!"

The German propagandists made up atrocity tales which the people read eagerly. These stories told how Belgians offered cigars filled with gunpowder to German soldiers. They charged that French priests gave coffee filled with poison to German troops.

The Allies had little trouble arousing hatred for the Germans. When the Germany army invaded Belgium, Belgian patriots "sniped" or shot at the troops from windows. In revenge, the German commanders took hostages — mayors, priests, women, children, anyone they could pick up. They said that unless the snipers were handed over to them, they would shoot every tenth person among the hostages. The whole world was horrified.

In addition, people in the Allied countries thought that German U-boat, or submarine, warfare was sneaky and cowardly. The Germans answered that everything was fair in war.

German "hate symbol" stamped on fuel blocks for use in the trenches. Translated, the words read, "God punish England"

Some of the propaganda was true, some very much exaggerated. For example, the Allies said that the Germans cut off the hands of babies and attacked women. They even said that the Germans boiled children in scalding water to get oil for their machines! This was not true, of course, but it helped people hate the Germans. This was what the propagandists wanted.

The Allies won the battle of propaganda. One of the main reasons why the United States entered the war on the side of the Allies in 1917 was the fact that the British were far better at propaganda than the Germans. Moreover, the Americans, with a sense of fair play, did not like the way the Germans were fighting the war.

Artist's conception of a German U-boat stopping a British ship

THE GERMAN U-BOAT CAMPAIGN

One of the things which particularly offended the Americans' sense of fair play was the German U-boat campaign.

Early in 1915 Germany announced a "war zone" of the waters around the British Isles. She said she would sink any enemy ships in this zone without warning. This was a violation of international law, which required that a ship be warned before it was sunk, and that every effort be made to save the lives of the passengers.

Germany argued that the U-boat was thin-shelled and easily destroyed by gunfire or ramming. It could be sunk by a single shot from an armed merchant ship. Therefore, it had to strike suddenly and secretly.

Shortly after their announcement of a war zone around Britain, the Germans began to use their U-boats to strike at Allied ships engaged in commerce.

German U-boats took a terrible toll of Allied ships. Sometimes they sank ships almost daily. Altogether these iron sharks of the sea sank five thousand Allied and neutral merchant and fishing ships during World War I.

Spectacular as this was, it did not succeed in starving out the British. Toward the end of the war the Allies worked out a system of convoys, by which merchant ships, guarded by sleek, fast destroyers, traveled together on the ocean lanes. This cut down the loss of ships.

Another method used by the Allies in fighting the U-boats was sending out innocent-looking merchant ships called Q-ships which could be changed into warships in a few seconds. These ships sailed along looking for all the world like unarmed freighters. Suddenly their sides went down, guns emerged, their real flag went up, and a U-boat was attacked.

The Germans used this trick, too, with great success. Their disguised ships were called raiders. In fifteen months the raider *Möwe* sank or captured thirty-eight Allied ships. Captain von Müller of the raider *Emden* destroyed seventy thousand tons of Allied shipping valued at 11 million dollars. But a British warship finally caught up with the *Emden* and sank her.

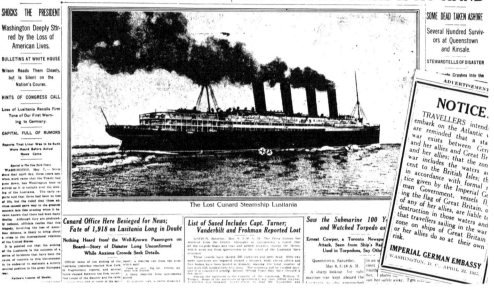

The New York Times masthead and front page content includes:

"All the News That's Fit to Print."

The New York Times.

EXTRA 5:30 A.M.

VOL. LXIV...NO. 20,928. NEW YORK, SATURDAY, MAY 8, 1915.—TWENTY-FOUR PAGES. ONE CENT

LUSITANIA SUNK BY A SUBMARINE, PROBABLY 1,260 DEAD; TWICE TORPEDOED OFF IRISH COAST; SINKS IN 15 MINUTES; CAPT. TURNER SAVED, FROHMAN AND VANDERBILT MISSING; WASHINGTON BELIEVES THAT A GRAVE CRISIS IS AT HAND

SHOCKS THE PRESIDENT

Washington Deeply Stirred by the Loss of American Lives.

BULLETINS AT WHITE HOUSE

Wilson Reads Them Closely, but Is Silent on the Nation's Course.

HINTS OF CONGRESS CALL

Loss of Lusitania Recalls Firm Tone of Our First Warning to Germany.

CAPITAL FULL OF RUMORS

Reports That Liner Was to be Sunk Were Heard Before Actual News Came.

SOME DEAD TAKEN ASHORE

Several Hundred Survivors at Queenstown and Kinsale.

STEWARD TELLS OF DISASTER

The Lost Cunard Steamship Lusitania

NOTICE.

TRAVELLERS intending to embark on the Atlantic voyage are reminded that a state of war exists between Germany and her allies and Great Britain and her allies; that the zone of war includes the waters adjacent to the British Isles; that, in accordance with formal notice given by the Imperial German Government, vessels flying the flag of Great Britain, or of any of her allies, are liable to destruction in those waters and that travellers sailing in the war zone on ships of Great Britain or her allies do so at their own risk.

IMPERIAL GERMAN EMBASSY
WASHINGTON, D. C., APRIL 22, 1915.

Front page of *The New York Times*, May 8, 1915. To the right is the advertisement placed in New York newspapers by the German Embassy

THE SINKING OF THE LUSITANIA

The *Lusitania,* a four-stacker of 30,395 tons, was the fastest ship afloat, the queen of the Cunard Line passenger fleet. She had left New York for Liverpool on May 1, 1915.

On that day the German Embassy in Washington had placed an advertisement in the New York newspapers warning that all ships flying the flag of Great Britain "are liable to destruction . . . and travellers sailing in the war zone . . . do so at their own risk."

46

No one paid any attention to this. It was unthinkable that the Germans would be foolish enough to sink a passenger ship with 197 Americans on board — and many women and children.

On Friday, May 7, the giant floating hotel was about ten miles off the coast of Ireland. Without warning, a torpedo crashed into her side. She trembled, her bow dipped forward, and she began to settle. There was panic as the desperate passengers and crew rushed to the lifeboats.

Captain Turner said: "I was on the bridge when I saw a torpedo speeding toward us. Immediately I tried to change our course, but was unable to maneuver out of the way. It was cold-blooded murder."

An eyewitness, a Dr. Moore of South Dakota, described it: "The *Lusitania* sank in just eighteen minutes. As she went down I saw a number of people jump from the topmost point of the deck into the sea. I heard no screaming at the last, but a long, wailing, mournful, despairing, beseeching cry."

And what did the U-boat commander, Lieutenant-Captain Schwieger, think? He reported in his log what he saw through his periscope: "Great confusion. . . . Lifeboats being cleared and lowered to water. . . . Many boats crowded. . . . I submerge to 24 meters and go to sea. I could not have fired a second torpedo into this throng of humanity struggling to save themselves."

There were 1,957 persons on board. Only 761 were saved. Of the 197 Americans, 128 lost their lives.

The German authorities claimed that the *Lusitania* was really a British warship, not a passenger vessel, and that she carried Canadian soldiers as well as huge supplies of ammunition and shrapnel shells. In Germany, the sinking was hailed as a great victory. School children were given a holiday, and a special medal was struck off to celebrate the event.

The tragedy sent a wave of mingled horror and anger through the United States. True, the *Lusitania* carried 4,200 cases of cartridges for rifles, and 1,250 cases of shrapnel. Yet it was never proved that she was armed. Most important of all, she carried defenseless men, women, and children. The sinking was clearly a violation of international law and the laws of humanity.

The *Lusitania* disaster, like the invasion of Belgium, hardened world opinion against Germany. It was one of the main reasons why the United States went to war.

A German U-boat

Italian Bersaglieri, members of a corps of expert riflemen belonging to the Italian Infantry

ITALY ENTERS THE WAR

In 1915 both the Allies and the Central Powers began to woo Italy. Germany promised her some Austrian soil after the war if she would join the Central Powers. The Allies, with nothing to lose, promised her even more Austrian territory, including the Tyrol, if she would join them. They also promised her Trieste, the Istrian peninsula, and a part of Dalmatia. Italy could, if she liked, make an "Italian lake" of the Adriatic Sea. Moreover, the Allies promised Italy colonies in Africa and a sphere of influence in Asiatic Turkey.

Many Italians were wildly excited by all this. On May 23, 1915, Italy joined the Allies.

THE GERMAN CONQUEST OF POLAND

Back in 1914, the Russians had driven the Austrian armies from Galicia, a Polish province then under Austrian control. In May, 1915, German artillery smashed at the Russian lines and sent them reeling.

The following August, just a year after the war began, the Germans surged on to Warsaw, the central point of the Polish railroad system. Hundreds of thousands of refugees choked the highways around the city. The retreating Russian troops, desperate to get away, shoved the refugees to their deaths in marshlands along the roads.

By winter the Germans had pushed the Russian armies back to the Pripet Marshes in West Russia. The Russians lost more than a million men and huge stocks of military equipment. They never recovered from that defeat. It was one of the reasons for the Russian revolutions of 1917.

Austrian and German cavalry crossing a temporary bridge over the Vistula River, Poland, in pursuit of the Russians

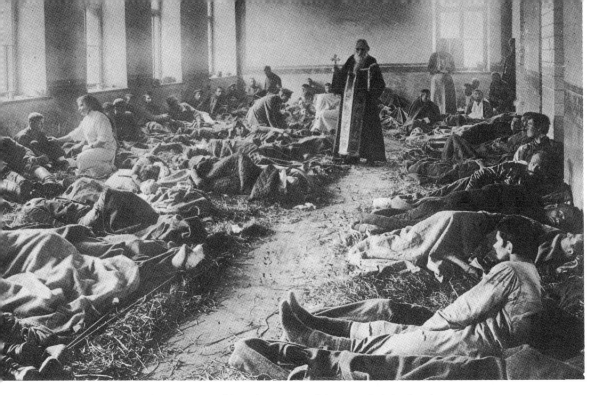

Wounded Russian soldiers being cared for in a Polish church

THE BALKANS AND THE NEAR EAST

With the Russians on the defensive and the British and French checked on all fronts, the German High Command believed that the time had come to destroy Serbia. They promised the Bulgarian king that if he made a flank attack on Serbia, they would make him over-lord of the Balkans.

The bribe worked. Bulgaria joined the Central Powers on October 8, 1915.

Three days later two great German and Austrian armies under the German General August von Mackensen swooped down on Serbia

51

from the north. Bulgarian troops came in from the east. Little Serbia was overcome. The Greeks, who had promised to help her, backed down.

The Central Powers were now triumphant from the North Sea to the Tigris River in Mesopotamia in the heart of the Near East. The road was open to Baghdad — and India.

In 1915 a British force from India invaded Mesopotamia and advanced as far as Kut-el-Amara. The idea was to take Baghdad and join up with the Russians. The little British army was almost overwhelmed by the Turks. The odds were too great — heat, exhaustion, lack of water at times, and floods at other times.

This British defeat was somewhat offset by a Russian invasion of Turkey from the northeast. In February, 1916, the Russians captured

King Peter, seated, watches the retreat of his armies

the Armenian city of Erzurum, then under Turkish control. The Turks knew that the Armenians wanted to be free of Turkish rule. They ordered a terrible massacre of the defenseless Armenians. Thousands of men, women, and children were driven into the desert, where they were butchered or died of famine. It was a pitiful story of man's inhumanity to man.

Further to the south in the Near East, British agents worked among the Arab chieftains, inciting them to rebel against their Turkish overlords. The most famous of these agents, one of the great resistance fighters of all time, was Colonel T. E. Lawrence, better known as Lawrence of Arabia.

A graduate of Oxford University, Lawrence was a gentle, shy archaeologist. When World War I began, he was digging up and studying the remains of past civilizations in the Near East. He had a vast knowledge of this area, especially of Arabia. Rejected by the British for military service because he was too short, he asked to be allowed to work with the Arabs.

And what important work he did! Promising the Arabs freedom after the war, he urged them to revolt against their Turkish masters. He led them in raids on trains and Turkish military installations. Lawrence had the full confidence of the Arabs. He knew their language. He dressed like them. He became "more Arab than the Arabs."

British cash and Arab lust for booty brought many of the Arab leaders to the Allied side. But the success of the Arab revolt was largely due to Colonel Lawrence, the little fighter whom the grateful Arabs called "El-Oren, the destroyer of engines."

One of the fortresses around Verdun

VERDUN

At the opening of the second year of the war, the Central Powers held all of Belgium and the industrial regions of France. In the East they had bottled up Russia. Now they decided to try to break the Allied line on the Western Front.

Overlooking the Meuse Valley in France is the city of Verdun. For years this city, surrounded by a triple ring of fortresses, had symbolized the power of France. The Germans knew that if they were to capture it, they would not only have a base for a fresh attack on Paris, but would seriously dishearten the French.

On February 21, 1916, began the epic battle of Verdun, one of the bloodiest chapters in the history of war. General Erich von Falkenhayn had secretly gathered the best of the German army in the area directly before Verdun. His plan was to smash the city with his big guns and then send in his foot soldiers: "The artillery conquers, the infantry occupies."

The Germans opened the campaign with the greatest bombardment ever known. Within the first twelve hours of battle they hurled more than a million shells from thousands of cannon against the French defenders. Then, behind a curtain of fire, the German infantry advanced.

The German High Command was delighted. A general announced, "We are fighting the last battle of the war!"

By June the Germans were only four miles from Verdun. The French commander-in-chief, General Joseph Joffre, or "Papa Joffre" as his troops called him, telegraphed to all his top field officers, "Every officer who gives an order to retreat will be tried by court-martial."

There had been doubts about the bravery of the French front-line soldiers. They were known as *poilus,* or "hairy ones," because they needed haircuts. Many people doubted their courage. But at Verdun they battled the German *Boches,* or "hard-heads," to the death. The more desperate the German attack, the more determined was the French defense.

The *poilus* shouted, *"Ils ne passeront pas!"* — "They shall not pass!"

Week after week, month after month, the bloodbath went on. In twenty square miles not a foot of ground was unburned by shellfire. The Germans even tried a new kind of poison gas — diphosgene — which penetrated the masks of the French defenders.

It was all in vain. The Germans did not take Verdun. Once again, as at the Marne, they were stopped. France was saved.

The cost was frightful. More than half a million men died in the raging battle. Neither the French nor the Germans ever fully recovered from this mass carnage. After Verdun, the British, and later the Americans, had to bear the main burden of the Allied fighting on French soil.

A German howitzer crew relaxes during a lull in the fighting on the Western Front

A French soldier patrols a long slit trench on the Somme River

THE BATTLE OF THE SOMME

While the Battle of Verdun was being fought, General Douglas Haig, the British commander-in-chief, raised a new army of volunteers. He planned to launch a tremendous counterattack on the Germans and relieve Verdun. At the same time, the Russians and Italians would strike at the Germans elsewhere.

General Haig concentrated 1,500 big guns, twenty yards apart, along the Somme River. At the end of June, 1916, the British began an eight-day heavy bombardment of the Germans, who were now under the command of General Paul von Hindenburg. In the early morning of July 1, the British infantry went "over the top."

For the first time in World War I, the German soldier was on the defensive against an enemy equipped with weapons equal to his own. Each day the British used more munitions than had been made in England during the whole first eleven months of the war.

When winter came, bad weather turned the fighting area into a sea of mud and blood. Neither side could make any headway. One British Tommy said, "It was the glory and graveyard of our army!"

When, after four months the fighting stopped, the British had conquered a small strip of soil thirty miles long and seven miles deep. But at what a cost! They lost 410,000 men.

The Battle of the Somme had two important results, however. It relieved the German pressure on Verdun, and it forced the Germans to retreat on a hundred-mile front running from east of Noyon to Arras in northeastern France.

British tanks

It was at the Battle of the Somme that the Allies introduced their answer to trench warfare.

One day at the battlefront — it was September 15, 1916 — some badly scared German soldiers saw a long, narrow steel monster coming at them. The huge vehicle *seemed* to have eight pairs of big wheels, each about ten feet in diameter. An astounded German officer wrote: "It did look something like a threshing machine. But why should it arrive there in the middle of a war? We watched and waited. Then it moved. It actually came toward us. But that was not all. Suddenly another came into view. Side by side they came on, ugly and ungainly, but terribly businesslike. Then, without warning, from both of them came a stream of bullets. Next they were on top of us."

These were the new British tanks. The idea was not new. Many

←

A British ammunition cart finds hard going through the mud on the Western Front centuries ago the Chinese used "war cars." And in Europe there had been talk about "battle wagons" and "land ships." But the tanks were more deadly than any such vehicle used before. They were really armored automobiles, using caterpillar tracks, which enabled them to move across soft ground, up and down hill, through barbed wire, and across the trenches. Meanwhile, they spat out smoke and bullets.

Before long the Germans began to build tanks, too. You will be interested in the name they gave their tanks. At first they called a tank a *Schützengrabenvernichtungsautomobile,* which means "An automobile built for the purpose of destroying trenches dug in the ground."

This word must have caused the Germans some trouble. Later they changed it to *Panzerwagen,* meaning "armored car."

THE BATTLE OF JUTLAND

Everyone wondered what would happen if the Grand Fleet of Great Britain and the High Seas Fleet of the German Empire ever clashed in battle. It finally happened on May 31-June 1, 1916 — in the only important naval battle of World War I. The fleets met in the North Sea, just off Jutland, the largest province of Denmark.

Word came to the British that the German fleet, under Admiral Reinhard Scheer, had just steamed out into the North Sea. Immediately the British fleet, under Admiral Sir John Jellicoe, headed out in the direction of the enemy.

Both sides used the same tactics. Each fleet divided itself into smaller ships (battle cruisers and destroyers) and a main battle fleet of giant battleships.

The British cruisers soon found the German cruisers, which at once turned away to rejoin their main fleet. There was a terrible battle as all the warships — big and little — skirted one another and rained steel at the enemy. Salvo after salvo fell on the decks. Ships exploded. Some, with great skill and agility, managed to dodge the torpedoes.

Gradually, the British ships worked their way to the east of the Germans, between them and their home ports. As soon as he was able to locate the enemy main fleet of battleships, Admiral Jellicoe, of the British fleet, formed a line of battle. The action between the two main battle fleets lasted just two hours.

The weather thickened as the day closed. Protected by destroyers, in a screen of gray smoke, the German fleet headed for its home base.

61

←

A tank crashes through a barbed wire entanglement

The Allies sink the German cruiser *Blücher* in the North Sea

When dawn came, on June 1, no German warships were to be seen.

There was no real "victory" for either side. The British lost three battle cruisers, three light cruisers, and eight destroyers. The Germans lost one battleship, one battle cruiser, four light cruisers, and five destroyers. The loss of life on some of the British ships was very great; nearly the entire crew of the *Queen Mary,* a battle cruiser, died when the ship exploded and sank.

Not since the rise of the British navy in the seventeenth century had the British been hurt so badly in a major naval battle. But still the Germans actually gained little in this great sea battle. The German High Seas Fleet retired to Kiel and stayed there for the rest of the war. Great Britain remained mistress of the seas.

RUMANIA JOINS THE ALLIES

There was a momentary flash to lighten the gloom that hung over the Allies in that black summer of 1916. For two years the Rumanians, in the southeastern corner of Europe, had bargained with both sides. In August, 1916, Rumania decided to join the Allied side.

The joy of the Allies did not last very long. The Rumanians invaded Transylvania, but their drive stalled. General Erich von Falkenhayn, at the head of the Austro-German forces, pushed the Rumanians out of Transylvania and turned on Rumania.

On December 6, 1916, Bucharest, the capital, fell. Rumania was subdued. She signed the humiliating Treaty of Bucharest, which cost her important strips of territory.

Now the priceless oil fields and the wheat harvest of Rumania were open to the Central Powers.

Rumanian prisoners, their feet wrapped in rags, beg for bread while their captor urges them forward

PEACE GESTURES

After two years of wasteful and expensive fighting both sides were tired of the war. The Allied world gloomily counted the costs of the bloodbaths of Verdun and the Somme. The Italian front was in a deadlock. Russia was about to explode into revolution. The Germans knew that the chances of victory now were small. And the many peoples inside the shaky Austro-Hungarian empire were restless and calling for peace.

On December 12, 1916, the German government issued a call for a negotiated peace — a peace on terms agreed to by both parties — in which neither side would win. It was an arrogant note, saying that the Germans had no wish to destroy their enemy. The Allies rejected it. Lloyd George, who had just become British Prime Minister, said, "We are not going to put our heads into a noose."

A few days later, the American President Woodrow Wilson, who had been working for peace since the beginning of the war, made a proposal for "peace without victory." He said, "Victory would mean peace forced upon the loser. Only a peace between equals can last."

But it was all in vain.

The bitterness portrayed on the faces of these German prisoners foreshadows the bitterness that was to grip all Germany after the war and help to bring Adolf Hitler into power

The Iron Cross, reward for bravery in the German Army

AMERICA ENTERS THE WAR

At the outbreak of war in 1914, the people of the United States had been hesitant and confused. America is made up of people whose families originally came from all over Europe. Many were in sympathy with the Allies. But there were also millions of Americans with a German background who felt close to the Fatherland. The Irish in America were anti-British because they felt that Ireland was oppressed by Britain. And the United States government protested strongly against such British practices as stopping American ships and using American flags to disguise British ships.

America immediately announced her neutrality. In doing so she was following George Washington's advice not to make "entangling alliances" with the European powers.

When the American presidential election took place in 1916, Wilson was returned to office on the slogan: *"He Kept Us Out of War."*

But gradually America began to turn against Germany. She was shocked by the way Germany fought the war, by her invasion of Belgium, her use of poison gas, her brutal bombing of cities, her sinking of defenseless ships. Again and again America warned the Germans to stop sinking United States ships.

The Germans also did many foolish things that aroused American resentment. They sent secret agents to the United States to blow up munitions factories and freight ships. Popular feeling flared high when German spies were accused of setting off a great explosion in the Black Tom munitions shipping terminals in New Jersey.

Then on January 19, 1917, the German Foreign Secretary, Alfred Zimmermann, did something that can be described only as stupid. He sent a note to the German Ambassador in Mexico, proposing an alliance with Mexico for a joint war against the United States. As a reward Mexico would be given territory in New Mexico, Texas, and Arizona. The note was intercepted and decoded by the British, handed to our Ambassador in London, Walter Hines Page, and then was published in the United States. You can imagine how the Texans reacted to that!

Then on January 29, 1917, the Germans announced to the world that they would begin unrestricted submarine warfare. Their U-boats would sink any ship on sight. One American ship after another was torpedoed and sunk.

The United States did not know how long the war would last. If the Germans drove her shipping from the seas, her business would disappear and she would become a pauper nation.

On April 6, 1917, America declared war against Germany.

The German reaction was shock and dismay. General von Hindenburg said, "We now have a new enemy. America is the most powerful country in the world. Will she appear in time to snatch the victor's laurel from our brow?"

The answer was "Yes!"

American troops arriving in London

At first only a few Yanks, as the American soldiers were called, crossed the ocean. But soon they came to Europe like an avalanche. Within a year more than two million men under the command of General John J. Pershing were sent to the battlefields of France. Never before in the history of the world had so many men been transported so far and supplied so well from bases thousands of miles away!

67

THE WESTERN FRONT, 1917

Following the Battle of the Somme, the Western Front remained deadlocked through 1917.

On April 9, 1917, the British struck at the northern tip of the Hindenburg Line. They prepared the way by three weeks of barbed-wire cutting followed by five days of heavy bombardment by nearly three thousand guns. Sixty tanks went into action. Canadian troops made a furious assault on Vimy Ridge, driving the Germans back several miles. But, at the end of two weeks the British had captured only seventy-five square miles at a cost of thirty thousand killed.

Meanwhile, the French started their own big offensive further south on the Hindenburg Line at a point between Soissons and Rheims. Here they received one of the bloodiest beatings of the war. Many French *poilus,* revolted by the massacre, threw down their weapons and went home. Some 150 were condemned to death for desertion, but only twenty-three were executed. Order was restored by changing the French leadership. General Robert Georges Nivelle was replaced by General Henri Pétain. Not only France but her allies were shaken by this disastrous defeat.

Then, on June 7, 1917, the British Second Army did an amazing thing. It dug a tunnel of eight thousand yards directly under the German trenches and exploded nineteen huge mines in it. Soon 2,300 heavy guns opened up. The British infantry swarmed in. But at the end of seven days this advance, too, was halted.

The British tried again at the Battle of Passchendaele in July, 1917.

Their guns poured more than four million shells on the Germans, but the enemy doggedly held its positions.

Once more, in November, the British went to the attack at the Battle of Cambrai. Here they used 380 tanks in a mighty offensive action. The battle was almost a victory for the British, but not quite. It came close to being a costly failure.

But, even if the year 1917 was a gloomy one and the war was a dirty mess, the British knew that they must endure and "muddle through."

Parisians anxiously watch an approaching airplane, not knowing whether it is friend or foe

RUSSIA WITHDRAWS FROM THE WAR

The United States entered the war none too soon. Russia was about to drop out.

To understand what happened in Russia in 1917, we must go back a few years. For a long time the Russian people had been on the verge of revolution. They were dissatisfied with the harsh rule of their czar. In late years their anger had been inflamed by the rise to power of an evil man named Grigoryi Efimovich, better known by his surname, Rasputin.

Rasputin

Rasputin was a half-mad peasant who could scarcely write his name. He had "gotten religion" and became a wandering "man of God," professing to have healing powers. He believed that the best way to conquer sin was to give in to it. His personal conduct was scandalous. Yet he had become the most powerful man in Russia.

The young heir to the throne of Russia, the Grand Duke Alexis, was a hemophiliac, or "bleeder." He bled profusely from even the smallest scratch, and the doctors could not stop it. The boy's mother, the Czarina, heard of Rasputin's healing powers. She called him in. The "holy man" would dangle a watch over the boy's eyes, mumble magic words, and tell him he was getting better.

Soon Rasputin became a court favorite. Then he began to meddle in politics. He even had ministers appointed and dismissed. The Russian people begged the Czar to throw him out.

70

Finally, in late 1916, three nobles decided to kill Rasputin. They fed him poisoned cakes and wine, but nothing happened. Then they shot him. To make sure he was dead, they threw his body under the ice of the Neva River.

But Rasputin's death came too late. All Russia was in chaos. The troops at the front, some fighting even without rifles, were about to mutiny. At home there was a serious shortage of food. Workers went on strike. Revolutionary feeling spread like wildfire. The Czar ordered troops to disperse the angry people, but the troops refused to fire on their fellow Russians. They even joined them.

On March 15, 1917, Czar Nicholas II gave up his throne. Sixteen months later he and his entire family were shot to death in a cellar by the revolutionists.

Following the abdication of the Czar, the revolutionists set up a Provisional, or temporary, Government under the leadership of Alexander Kerensky. It was more or less a democracy. The Allies were delighted. Now they could say they were really fighting to "make the world safe for democracy."

The Provisional Government tried to continue the war on the side of the Allies. But the Russian masses, tired of military blundering and the heavy losses at the front, turned against it.

Meanwhile, a lonely exile in Switzerland watched his hour of destiny approach. He was called Lenin, but that was not his real name. His true name was Vladimir Ilyich Ulyanov. He was a person consumed with hatred for the Russian government that long ago had executed his older brother as a radical. He had long planned to have his revenge.

The Germans wanted revolution in Russia so that one of their enemies would be out of the fight. They allowed Lenin to cross Germany from Switzerland in a sealed train.

Lenin arrived in Russia on April 16, 1917. He declared that the overthrow of the Czar was only the beginning of the revolution. The Provisional Government, he said, represented the middle class or *bourgeoisie* — capitalists such as businessmen, doctors, lawyers, and teachers. He demanded all power for the working class, or *proletariat*. His slogan — *Peace! Land! Bread!* — became a battle cry for the downtrodden workers and peasants.

At this time Lenin's party was called the Bolsheviks. It was small but well organized. It had able leaders. In November, 1917, it staged a second great revolution — "the ten days that shook the world." The

Revolutionists barricade the streets of Petrograd (once St. Petersburg)

Bolsheviks overthrew Kerensky and set up what Lenin called a "Dictatorship of the Proletariat." Actually, it was the dictatorship of one man — Lenin. The Russians had exchanged one tyrant for another.

Once in power, the Bolsheviks signed a treaty of peace with the Germans. With the harsh treaty of Brest-Litovsk, March 3, 1918, the Russians gave to Germany nearly all the territory they had acquired in Eastern Europe since the time of Peter the Great (1672-1725).

The Allies were stunned by this desertion. German troops were now released from the Russian front to fight in France. There was great danger that unless the fighting was brought to a speedy end, all of war-exhausted Europe would give in to the Bolsheviks, who were preaching world revolution.

← Lenin speaking to a crowd in Petrograd during the Bolshevik Revolution

THE HOLY CITY

The disastrous year of 1917 held one bright moment for the Allies. Their campaign against the Turks ended in victory. In early 1917 British troops under General F. Stanley Maude captured Baghdad in Mesopotamia. Later that same year another British army under General Edmund Allenby joined up with the Arab guerrillas under Lawrence at Damascus in Turkish Syria. The combined forces then marched into Jerusalem just before Christmas, 1917. For the first time since the Crusades (1095-1270) the Holy City was returned to Christian possession.

DISASTER AT CAPORETTO

In late 1917, this time from southern Europe, more bad news came to the Allies.

Some Italians believed that they should not have entered the war at all. Italy, they said, had no coal, without which no nation could fight a modern war. Once in the war the people had little or no will to win. The Italian soldier had no stomach for fighting.

Nevertheless, in 1916 the Italian armies began hammering away at the mountainous borders of Austria-Hungary.

Suddenly, on October 24, 1917, with no warning, a huge combined German and Austrian army swept down on Caporetto, in northeastern Italy. Within two weeks the entire Italian line crumbled. The defenders were thrown back to the Piave River, a mere fifteen miles from the canals of Venice.

The Battle of Caporetto was a complete rout for Italy, a disaster for the Allies. The Italian armies turned into a mob desperately trying to save itself. The roads were so clogged with fleeing people that even a fighting army could not have retreated in order.

British and French troops were hurriedly sent in to bolster the sagging Italian front. The defeat at Caporetto stung the pride of a fiercely sensitive people, already resentful of the world's criticism. Young Italian boys of seventeen and eighteen were rushed to the front lines. They fought well alongside veteran British and French troops. Some of the lost ground was regained. But Italy never fully recovered from the crippling blow at Caporetto.

75

←

A group of German soldiers celebrate Christmas Eve in a shelter on the Western Front.

THE CRITICAL YEAR: 1918

Early in the critical year of 1918 the Central Powers *seemed* to be in a favorable position. Some two million Germans defended the Hindenburg Line on the Western Front. Russia was out of the war. Serbia, Rumania, and Italy were no longer important as military powers. The U-boat campaign was working havoc on Allied shipping. England was facing starvation. No one knew if the Americans were ready to face the German veterans.

Then it came — the expected German super-offensive.

On March 21, 1918, the German armies, under Generals Hindenburg and Ludendorff, surged forward. The plan was to end the war by a series of hammer strokes before the Americans could arrive in overwhelming numbers. The Allies lost 1,500 square miles which they had won only after three years of bloody fighting.

For the first time in the war the Allies agreed to work together under a single command. General Ferdinand Foch, a Frenchman, was named Supreme Commander of all the Allied Forces. No longer would there be petty bickering among the Allied commanders.

On April 4, 1918, the Germans struck again against the British lines to the north. Another such push and the Channel ports, so vital for the safety of England, would be captured.

Then the Germans turned on the French at the southern end of the Hindenburg Line. Their hammer strokes carried them forward again to the Marne River. They were on the verge of victory when the Americans began to arrive at the front.

A French machine gun unit in a first-line trench on the Western Front

Now a great Allied counter-offensive was prepared all along the line. The idea was to give the Germans no rest, to attack them first at one section of the line and then at another. The big push came in July, 1918. The British struck at the north on their old battlefield, the Somme. Slowly but surely they forced the Germans out of all the positions they had gained since March.

Further to the south, from Amiens to Rheims, the French pushed the Germans back to their original line. This great Second Battle of the Marne (July 15-August 8, 1918) was a resounding Allied victory.

General Ludendorff said, "August 8 was the black day of the German army. It put the decline of our fighting power beyond all doubt."

Next came the great assault on the Hindenburg Line. Here the raw

American troops go "over the top" in France

American troops distinguished themselves. The Germans dropped back into the Argonne Forest, a wooded region and rocky plateau in the Meuse and Ardennes region of France. Some of the most desperate fighting of the war followed.

And here, in the Argonne Forest, there took place one of the most glorious episodes of American military history — the advance and rescue of the Lost Battalion. On the night of October 2, 1918, a battalion of the American 77th Division, commanded by Major Charles Whittlesey, took part in an attack on a German position deep in the forest. Advancing in single file, the Americans gained their objective. But at dawn they found Germans entrenched in front, behind, and on both sides of their position.

Surrounded by the enemy, the Americans were plastered with heavy gunfire and machine gun bullets. They had no food for thirty-six hours. But they held out against the enemy for five days. They were rescued on October 7.

The Allied armies pushed ahead along the entire front. The Hindenburg Line caved in completely. The German horde staggered back, unable to make a stand. Their generals, blaming "fresh American troops" for their defeat, secretly warned the Berlin government that the war was lost.

Men of the 23rd Infantry, U.S.A., fire a 37-millimeter gun at a German position

"Calamity Jane," the gun that fired the last shot on the American side in World War I

→

The railroad car in which the Germans signed the armistice ending World War I

One by one the Central Powers collapsed. Bulgaria surrendered on September 30, 1918. Turkey gave up on October 31. Austria-Hungary surrendered on November 3.

During this time the German home front began to fall apart. The people were shocked by their huge losses on the battlefield. Every family had lost a father, a son, or a relative. There was little to eat. The people lived mostly on turnips — bread made of turnips, coffee made of turnips, soup made of turnips, cigarettes made of turnips. They could scarcely look a turnip in the face!

As the avenging Allied armies approached the German frontier, the Germans finally gave up. The armistice was signed on November 11, 1918, aboard a railroad car in the forest of Compiègne. Remember that spot! A little over twenty years later, in 1940, at the beginning of World War II, Adolf Hitler humiliated the French with a vice-versa surrender at exactly the same place, using the very same railroad car. It was a piece of planned revenge. Adolf Hitler had been a corporal in World War I.

THE FOURTEEN POINTS AND THE SECRET TREATIES

On January 8, 1918, President Wilson had announced the famous Fourteen Points, a statement of America's war aims. They were:

1. Abolition of secret diplomacy.
2. Freedom of the seas.
3. Equality of trade for all nations.
4. Reduction of armaments.
5. Adjustment of colonial aims.
6. Evacuation of Russian territory.
7. Restoration of Belgium.
8. Return of Alsace-Lorraine to France.
9. Readjustment of the frontiers of Italy on the basis of nationality.
10. Freedom for the peoples of Austria-Hungary.
11. Evacuation of Serbia, Montenegro, and Rumania.
12. Freedom for the peoples subjugated by Turkey.
13. An independent Polish state.
14. Establishment of a League of Nations.

It is important to remember that thoughts and words are also weapons in war. Wilson's Fourteen Points were shot at the enemy by rockets and guns, scattered from planes and balloons, and broadcast (for the first time) by radio. The Germans took them seriously. Later, they said bitterly that they had been fooled. They had put down their arms, they said, because of Wilson's promise of a better world.

The Fourteen Points won the greatest diplomatic victory of World War I.

Starving Berliners salvage potatoes from a garbage dump as the war draws to a close

But remember that the Fourteen Points were *American* aims. Unfortunately, America's Allies had other plans. After the war, the Russian Bolsheviks, who were anxious to embarrass the capitalist powers, revealed the existence of secret treaties among the Allies (America did not make any of these treaties). Russia was to get Constantinople and the territory on the Straits. Italy was promised chunks of Austria. Russia, England, France, and Italy were to split Turkey among themselves. The German colonies were to be divided.

There was going to be great trouble in making a peace for a war-torn world. On the one side were the Fourteen Points with their aim of making a better world. And on the other were those secret treaties which could only lead to further war.

THE PEACE OF VERSAILLES, 1919

"Vive Vil-son!" cried the French in Paris.

"Hurrah for Wilson!" shouted the crowds in London.

"Viva Voovro Veelson!" screamed the mobs in Rome.

Everywhere it was the same — endless cheers and cries that seemed to come from the heart of humanity. For the first time in American history an American President had traveled to Europe during his term of office. He had come to lead the world to a just peace. He told the cheering multitudes:

"The cause being just and holy, the settlement must be of like quality. A supreme moment of history has come. The eyes of the people have been opened and they see. The hand of God is upon the nations."

The terrible war was over. Europe was a shambles. The people were exhausted and insecure. They looked upon President Wilson as a messiah to lead them from a world of decay.

Things went wrong from the start. Thirty-two Allied nations gathered to dictate terms to the defeated Central Powers. There was a bad omen in the very place they picked to make the treaty. It was the Hall of Mirrors in the Palace of Versailles, near Paris. Here, forty-eight years earlier, the Germans, after defeating the French, had proclaimed their German Empire. Already there was revenge in the air at Versailles.

The "Big Three" were President Woodrow Wilson, Premier Georges Clemenceau of France, and Prime Minister David Lloyd George of

England. Clemenceau was called the "Old Tiger of France," although he looked more like a walrus than a tiger. He hated Germany, which he regarded as a sinful nation. "When I die," he said, "bury me deep, standing up, marching toward Germany." The Germans could expect no mercy from him.

Lloyd George, the British Prime Minister, had just been re-elected to office on the slogan, "Hang the Kaiser!" He promised his people that he would collect from Germany the costs of the war, "shilling for shilling, and ton for ton."

David Lloyd George (England), Vittorio Orlando (Italy) Georges Clemenceau (France), and Woodrow Wilson (United States) at the time of the signing of the Versailles Treaty

The conference at Versailles was called "a riot in a parrot house." There were battles galore between the Big Three. Clemenceau was bored by Wilson. Of Wilson's Fourteen Points he said, "Wilson has Fourteen; the Good Lord Himself had only Ten!" The constant bickering shattered Wilson's nerves. He caught cold from Clemenceau, who coughed all the time. And Lloyd George was disgusted. "What am I to do," he asked, "between a man who thinks he is Jesus Christ and another who thinks he is Napoleon?"

Wilson had one first aim in mind — there must be a League of Nations to prevent another world war in the future. He reluctantly accepted some of the harsher terms of the treaty in return for support of his League of Nations.

And a hard peace it was! At Versailles the Allies stripped Germany of all her colonies in Africa and the Far East. Alsace-Lorraine was returned to France. The new state of Poland was created, part of it running in a corridor right through old German lands. The Saar territory, sometimes called the Pittsburgh of Germany, with all its coal mines and factories, was placed under French control for fifteen years. The German Rhineland was occupied by the victor powers for the same period.

Article 231 of the Treaty of Versailles, the famous war-guilt clause, formally blamed Germany and her allies alone for causing the war. On the basis of this clause, the Germans were required to pay an enormous amount of money and goods, called reparations. They did not want to pay and they could not pay. Reparations were stopped at the Treaty of Lausanne in 1932 by the Allies and never resumed.

The Allies made sure that Germany would be too weak to fight another war. Her army was limited to one hundred thousand men. Her navy was cut to six battleships, six light cruisers, twelve destroyers, and twelve torpedo boats. She could no longer have any submarines or make poison gas. She had to demolish all her fortifications.

Wilhelm II, the German Kaiser, who had abdicated and escaped to Holland, and other major German leaders were to be tried as war criminals (they never were). Everything possible was done to humiliate the defeated country.

The Germans protested heatedly against this treaty, but they could do nothing about it. On June 28, 1919, a reluctant German delegation signed the document.

Surrender of the German U-boats at Scapa Flow

The Germans took their loss with great bitterness. On June 21, 1919, they sailed their fleet of warships into Scapa Flow, the British naval base in the Orkneys, where it was to be surrendered. The German sailors opened the sea-cocks of their ships. Some fifty-three vessels went to the bottom. This was the German way of showing their contempt for the victors.

The Germans were also supposed to return to France the French flags captured in battle in 1870-1871. A group of officers and students in Berlin burned these flags before the statue of Frederick the Great, the Prussian hero-king of the eighteenth century.

Harsh treaties similar to that of Versailles were also imposed on the other losers — on Austria, Hungary, Bulgaria, and Turkey.

So it went. Crowns rolled in the gutter, ancient tyrannies were broken. Four imperial governments were swept away — Germany, Austria-Hungary, Russia, and Turkey.

At the same time a wave of republicanism washed over Europe. In 1914 there were only five republics — France, Switzerland, Portugal, San Marino, and Andorra. Eighteen years later there were sixteen republics on the continent.

Even though people hoped that the world really would be made safe for democracy, this was not the case. In healing the old scars, the peacemakers made new wounds. New military alliances were formed. Europe was divided once more into hostile camps.

Three new political experiments got under way — Bolshevism in Russia, Mussolini's Fascism in Italy, and Hitler's Nazism in Germany. Each one was a new deadly danger for an unhappy world.

EUROPE, 1919

THE COST OF WORLD WAR I

"Not until our children's time," said one general after the war, "can the former joy of life come into the world."

During the four years of World War I about ten million men died in action or of wounds. Think of this! That was twice as many men as were killed in all the major wars from 1790 to 1913.

And that was not all. More than twenty-one million men were

War brought starvation to these children. Here they are receiving soup and doughnuts from a relief agency

wounded, about a third of them permanently disabled. Six million men were taken prisoners, or were reported as missing. No record was ever kept of the number of war orphans, widows, and refugees. You can well imagine the effects of this mass tragedy — disease, epidemics, starvation, and the loss of young manhood.

Human casualties cannot be replaced. You cannot reckon human life in terms of money. Think of the great material losses — damage to property, the cost of munitions and weapons of war, and losses in shipping. This amounted to more than $300 billion. That was five and a half times as many dollars as the number of seconds which had passed since the birth of Christ!

This was an enormous amount of money, even in terms of 1918 dollars. Let us do some figuring with it. Do you know what it could have bought? (From *Scholastic,* November 10, 1934)

1. It would have given *every family* in England, France, Belgium, Germany, Russia, the United States, Canada, and Australia a $2,500 house on a $500 one-acre lot, with $1,000 worth of furniture, *and*

2. It would have given a library worth $5 million to every community of about 200,000 inhabitants in those countries, *and*

3. It would have set up a fund that would yield enough interest to pay $1,000 a year to 125,000 teachers and 125,000 nurses for an indefinite period, *and*

4. It would still leave enough to replace the entire wealth of France and Belgium.

Instead of this, World War I scraped Europe bare. No wonder intelligent men, horrified by the costs, said, "It must not happen again!"

THE LEAGUE OF NATIONS

The Treaty of Versailles had many failures, but it contained one thing which promised to bring justice among peoples, and might some day end all wars — the League of Nations.

The League of Nations was a kind of parliament or Congress of the whole world. It aimed to promote co-operation among nations, and to achieve peace by bringing relations between nations into the open, by enforcing international law, and insuring respect for all treaty obligations.

From its very beginning the League of Nations faced many difficulties. One of the most important reasons for this was that the United States would not join it. When President Wilson returned home from Paris he fought hard for the League, but the United States Senate would not support it. Even though the United States had just fought in what had started as a European war, a group of Senators called "isolationists" insisted that she must keep out of European affairs.

President Wilson traveled through the country, begging the American people to support him. "If we do not join the League," he said, "I can predict with absolute certainty that within another generation there will be another world war."

After delivering his fortieth speech at Pueblo, Colorado, he collapsed from nervous and physical exhaustion.

Wilson was absolutely right. Twenty years later began an even greater and more horrible World War.

After World War I, a famous British writer, G. Lowes Dickinson,

92

→

French children playing in the rubble of their bombed home

said, "This much is certainly true, that until men lay down their arms, and accept the method of peaceable decision of their disputes, wars can never cease."

He, too, like President Wilson, was right. What he meant was that *all* nations must lay down their arms.

It is a most important lesson. All the nations of the world must get rid of their selfish national feelings and work together in the interests of a common humanity. This is our only hope.

WORLD WAR I WORDS

ACE: A World War I aviator who shot down at least five enemy planes in combat over his own lines.

ANZAC: A member of the Australian and New Zealand Army Corps, or the Corps itself.

BIG BERTHA: Slang for any German gun of large bore and long range, named after Frau Bertha Krupp von Bohlen and Halbach, head of the Krupp steel works.

BOCHE: Nickname for the German soldier; from the French *caboche,* meaning "hard head."

BOOBY TRAP: A concealed grenade or mine set to explode when disturbed.

CONTRABAND OF WAR: According to international law, any war goods that could not be supplied to one nation except at the risk of seizure by an enemy nation.

COOTIE: A body louse highly unpopular among World War I soldiers.

COSSACK: From Russian *kazak,* a cavalry fighter of the Russian steppes.

DOG FIGHT: A general mix-up of World War I planes, with each trying to down enemy planes.

DOLLAR -A -YEAR MEN: American business men who worked for the Government for pay of a dollar a year.

DOUGHBOY: Slang for an American infantryman.

DRANG NACH OSTEN: The German effort to gain control of the Near and Middle East.

DREADNOUGHT or DREADNAUGHT: A British battleship of 17,000 tons, completed in 1906-1907, having an armament of ten 12-inch guns and twenty-four 12-pound quick-firing guns. Later applied to any battleship having as its main armament big guns all of one calibre.

FLYING CIRCUS: Baron von Richthofen's fighter-pilots.

HINDENBURG LINE: The heavily fortified line to which the Germans retreated on the Western Front.

HUNS: Name used by Allied propagandists to describe the Germans, after the barbarous Asiatic Huns who invaded the Roman Empire in the middle of the 5th century.

ITALIA IRREDENTA: "Italy unredeemed," areas of Austria-Hungary and France bordering Italy which claimed that they were Italian.

JERRY: British nickname for a German soldier; from the word *German.*

KAMERAD!: German word meaning "Comrade!" Used by German troops raising their arms in surrender.

LIBERTY BONDS: U.S. war bonds sold in World War I.

NO-MAN'S-LAND: A belt of ground between the most advanced trenches of opposing armies.

OVER THE TOP: Leaving the trenches for an attack against the enemy.

POILU: A first-line French soldier; from the French word *poilu,* meaning hairy; suggested by the infantryman's uncut hair.

Q-SHIPS: Ships disguised as merchant vessels; used to lure U-boats to destruction.

SCHLIEFFEN PLAN: German plan before 1914 to fight a two-front war against France and Russia.

"SPURLOS VERSENKT!": "Sunk Without a Trace!" German way of reporting a U-boat sinking.

THRIFT STAMPS: Stamps bought to help the American war effort; could be changed into Liberty Bonds.

TOMMY ATKINS: From *Thomas* Atkins, a fictitious name used as a model in official blank forms for private soldiers of the British Army.

U-BOAT: *Untersee Boot,* or Undersea Boat, a German submarine.

ULTIMATUM: Final terms offered by either party in a diplomatic dispute.

YANK: Name applied by foreigners and also Americans to the American soldier.

ZERO HOUR: British military term; the hour at which a planned attack got under way.

94

INDEX

The number of books that may be
drawn at one time by the card holder
is governed by the reasonable needs of
the reader and the material on hand.

Books for junior readers are subject
to special rules.